MATCH OF THE **DAY**

Match Of The Day
ANNUAL 2014

This annual belongs to: Aron Logan

Age: 11

My favourite team is: celtic

My favourite player is: commons

My highlight of 2013 was: celtic wining
the league

WELCOME!

> Wow, what a year of football that was, and next year is set to be even more epic! So, take a seat, put your feet up and enjoy your Match Of The Day Annual 2014. But, remember, folks, football is for life, not just for Christmas!

2013: a quick reminder!

So, Man. United won their 20th league title ● Robin Van Persie was top scorer ● **Wigan won the FA Cup** ● Gareth Bale pipped Luis Suarez to PFA Player Of The Year, mainly because Suarez bit Branislav Ivanovic, and then signed for Real Madrid ● **Ivanovic helped Chelsea win the Europa League** ● The Champions League final was an all-German affair won by an amazing Bayern Munich team ● **And we waved goodbye to a legend – the one and only Sir Alex Ferguson!**

THIS BOOK IS NOT SUITABLE FOR...

OAPs!

MR BEAN!

CRICKET FANS!

MINIONS

WHAT'S INSIDE

WHAT'S NOT INSIDE

Is Wayne Rooney going bananas? p10

The player who thinks he's a toilet brush!

Is Cristiano Ronaldo better than a chip? p58

The world's worst defender!

What do Jack Wilshere and Gareth Bale have in common? p60

EastEnders chumpster Ian Beale!

Is this man the future of football? p74

The old one from The Apprentice!

What was Lionel Messi really like at school? p84

PLUS loads, loads more!

Cbeebies fluff-heads Big & Small!

LOUIS WALSH!

DALEKS!

DOGS WHO THINK THEY'RE HUMAN!

QUICK! Turn over now before Luis Suarez nibbles your fingers off!

BARCLAYS

2014 IS ALL ABOUT JACK!

Once every million years something comes along that takes your breath away. We're thinking dinosaurs, unicorns and Tangfastics. But there's another thing to add to that list – Jack Wilshere. The Arsenal and England youngster can become the world's top midfielder in 2014!

THE MAKING OF A LEGEND!

Whatever you do, believe the hype – because this kid is the real deal!

THE ENGLISH SPANIARD!
It's not just the Spanish who produce nimble, silky-skilled ball-players. Jack's got all that in his locker!

ARSENAL v BARCELONA
When the Gunners met Barca in 2011, midfield kings Xavi and Iniesta were both left chasing Jack's shadow!

ENGLAND v BRAZIL
When Brazil rocked up at Wembley all eyes were on Neymar – but it was our Jack who stole the show!

IF CLUBS WERE POPSTARS!

Man. United would be...
JUSTIN BIEBER
Successful, loved by millions – but could go off the rails in 2014!

Liverpool would be...
THE ROLLING STONES
Big fanbase but not been No.1 for years and keep mentioning the old days!

Chelsea would be...
JAY Z
Supremely talented, and totally loaded – but not everybody's cup of tea!

TOP 5
ENGLISH INVENTIONS

1
The internet
Just imagine a world without it. Think about it. Go on! How rubbish would that be?
Invented: 1980

Jack Wilshere
Maybe not as ground-breaking as the internet – but a million times better at passing!
Invented: 1992
2

3
The pencil
They don't just grow on trees, you know. Invented by a farmer 500 years ago!
Invented: 1500

The Scotch Egg
How do they even get the egg in there? A ridiculous idea that works a treat!
Invented: 1738
4

5
Fizzy pop
When those bubbles go up your nose or make you burp, thank Joseph Priestley!
Invented: 1767

Arsenal would be...
EMINEM
Loads of cash and style – but can't reach the heights of a decade ago!

Man. City would be...
ONE DIRECTION
Exploded onto the scene in 2010 – but it could all end in the blink of an eye!

THE WORLD'S WORST PITCH!

RVP!

Ruthless Vintage Predator

Your guide to the Premier League's No.1 striker!

How he scored his league goals 2012-13

RVP scores when he wants

The Arsenal fans were telling us that ages ago. He's bagged 89 goals in the last three years, he's been the Prem top scorer for the past two seasons and hit 35 goals in 76 games for Holland!

LEFT FOOT	18
RIGHT FOOT	6
HEADERS	2

Van Persie: his story!

DUTCH DESTROYER!

RVP started his career as a left-winger at Feyenoord, in Holland, before moving to Arsenal for just £2.75m in 2004. That's when Arsene Wenger converted him into a deadly striker!

GUNNERS LEGEND!

In eight seasons at Arsenal, the only trophy he won was the FA Cup – but he was voted Premier League Player Of The Year and was twice named Arsenal Player Of The Year!

FAMILY GUY!

His £22.5 million switch to Man. United in 2012 meant he had to move north. He now lives in Cheshire, eight miles from Old Trafford, with his wife Bouchra and children, Shaqueel and Dina!

Who's the real David Luiz?

1

2

3

4

SCHOOL FOOTY XI

Your simple guide to who's who!

The last to be picked!

His dad's got a tractor!

Class clown!

Can kick the ball miles!

Too slow to be a winger!

Ridiculously fast!

Best player – and he knows it!

Teacher's pet!

Skilful – but lazy!

Always doing his hair!

Goal hanger!

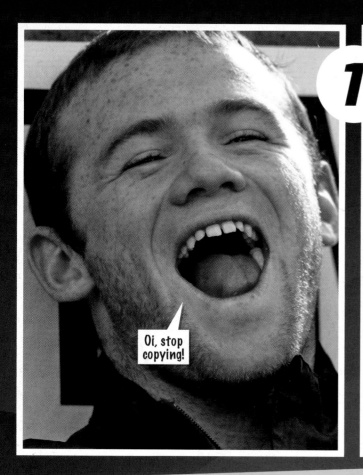

8 orangutans that look like Wayne Rooney

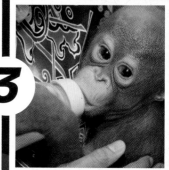

Seriously, give it a rest!

Nah, you give it a rest!

Aw, this is ridiculous!

Tee-hee!

FOOTY PIE CHARTS

Did someone say pie?

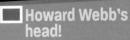
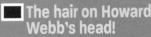

- [ ] Howard Webb's head!
- [x] The hair on Howard Webb's head!

- [ ] The money in Arsene Wenger's piggy bank!
- [ ] How much he wants to spend!

- [ ] What Sepp Blatter knows about footy!
- [x] What he doesn't know about footy!

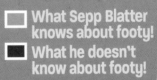

OI, EVERYBODY, LOOK AT THIS MUG!

THIS IS LIVERPOOL

BUT WHY HAS HE GOT A LIVERPOOL CUP?

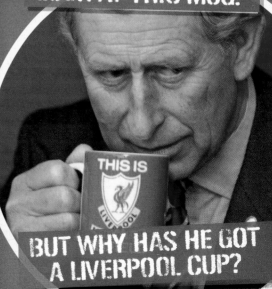

TRUE OR FALSE?

10 POINTS for each right answer!

Some of these outrageous statements are true – can you work out which ones?

1 Petr Cech is the owner of Prague Badger Farm, which helps abandoned badgers!

TRUE ☐ — FALSE ✓

2 Tottenham boss **AVB** was the European Under-11 Scrabble champion in 1988!

TRUE ✓

FALSE ☐

3 Ex-Chelsea manager Rafa Benitez invented the sausage when he was growing up in Spain!

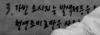

TRUE ☐

✓ FALSE

4 During his time in Manchester, Cristiano Ronaldo was addicted to playing bingo!

TRUE ☐

✓ FALSE

5 Rio Ferdinand was a ballet dancer when he was a kid!

TRUE ✓

FALSE ☐

MY SCORE

☐ OUT OF **50**

ANSWERS ON p92

TURN TO p42 FOR MORE QUIZ ACTION!

NEYMAR
BARCELONA

FUNNIES

Erm, alakazam?

Whoa!

All those hours at Hogwarts finally paid off for Yaya...

Del Bosque: The man with one face!

Spain win...

Spain draw...

Spain lose...

Too sour. Next!

Becks had always wondered what they tasted like...

THEO WALCOTT
ARSENAL

THE
TOP TEN
OF EVERYTHING YOU EVER WANTED TO KNOW ABOUT FOOTBALL!

FEATURING

EUROPE'S SUPERCLUBS

THE BIGGEST LEGENDS

ENORMOUS STADIUMS

MIND-BLOWIN' STATS & FACTS

MEGA FACTS IMPRESS YOUR MATES WITH YOUR TOP KNOWLEDGE!

TOP TENS

Which is the biggest stadium in the Prem?

1	Old Trafford	Man. United	75,765
2	Emirates	Arsenal	60,362
3	St James' Park	Newcastle	52,405
4	Stadium Of Light	Sunderland	48,707
5	Etihad Stadium	Man. City	47,405
6	Anfield	Liverpool	45,276
7	Villa Park	Aston Villa	42,786
8	Stamford Bridge	Chelsea	41,798
9	Goodison Park	Everton	40,157
10	White Hart Lane	Tottenham	36,284

Which English club has won the most league titles?

1	Man. United	20
2	Liverpool	18
3	Arsenal	13
4	Everton	9
5	Aston Villa	7
6	Sunderland	6
7=	Sheff. Wed	4
	Newcastle	
	Chelsea	
10=	Man. City	3
	Wolves	
	Leeds	
	Huddersfield	
	Blackburn	

Which club has won the most points in Premier League history?

1	Man. United	1752 points
2	Arsenal	1522 points
3	Chelsea	1477 points
4	Liverpool	1395 points
5	Tottenham	1158 points
6	Aston Villa	1130 points
7	Everton	1097 points
8	Newcastle	1058 points
9	Blackburn	970 points
10	Man. City	862 points

Correct up to the end of the 2012-13 season

Which club has won the most FA Cups?

1	Man. United	11 wins
2	Arsenal	10 wins
3	Tottenham	8 wins
4=	Liverpool	7 wins
	Chelsea	
	Aston Villa	
7=	Newcastle	6 wins
	Blackburn	
9=	Everton	5 wins
	West Brom	
	Man. City	

Which club has won the most League Cups?

1	Liverpool	8 wins
2	Aston Villa	5 wins
3=	Chelsea	4 wins
	Man. United	
	Nott'm Forest	
	Tottenham	
7	Leicester	3 wins
8=	Arsenal	2 wins
	Birmingham	
	Man. City	
	Norwich	
	Wolves	

Which is the biggest stadium in the Football League?

1	Hillsborough	Sheff. Wed.	39,732
2	Elland Road	Leeds	37,914
3	Riverside Stadium	Middlesbrough	34,998
4	Pride Park Stadium	Derby	33,502
5	Bramall Lane	Sheff. United	32,609
6	King Power Stadium	Leicester	32,312
7	Ewood Park	Blackburn	31,154
8	Molineux	Wolves	30,852
9	The Amex	Brighton	30,750
10	City Ground	Nott'm Forest	30,540

What is the biggest win in Premier League history?

1	Man. United 9-0 Ipswich	March 1995
2	Tottenham 9-1 Wigan (pictured)	November 2009
3=	Newcastle 8-0 Sheffield Wednesday	September 1999
	Chelsea 8-0 Wigan	May 2010
5	Chelsea 8-0 Aston Villa	December 2012
6=	Nott'm Forest 1-8 Man. United	February 1999
	Middlesbrough 8-1 Man. City	May 2008
8=	Man. United 7-0 Barnsley	October 1997
	Arsenal 7-0 Everton	May 2005
	Arsenal 7-0 Middlesbrough	January 2006
	Blackburn 7-0 Nottingham Forest	November 1995
	Chelsea 7-0 Stoke	April 2010

Correct up to the end of the 2012-13 season

Which is the oldest club in England?

1	Notts County	151 years old
2	Stoke	150 years old
3	Nott'm Forest	148 years old
4=	Sheffield Wednesday	146 years old
	Chesterfield	
6	Rotherham	143 years old
7	Reading	142 years old
8	Colchester	140 years old
9=	Aston Villa	139 years old
	Bolton	

What is the biggest transfer of all time

1	Gareth Bale	£85m	Tottenham to Real Madrid (2013)
2	Cristiano Ronaldo	£80m	Man. United to Real Madrid (2009)
3	Zlatan Ibrahimovic	£59m	Inter Milan to Barcelona (2009)
4	Kaka	£56m	AC Milan to Real Madrid (2009)
5	Edinson Cavani	£55m	Napoli to PSG (2013)
6	Radamel Falcao	£51m	Atletico Madrid to Monaco (2013)
7=	Neymar	£50m	Santos to Barcelona (2013)
	Fernando Torres	£50m	Liverpool to Chelsea (2011)
9	Zinedine Zidane	£46m	Juventus to Real Madrid (2001)
10	Mesut Ozil	£42m	Real Madrid to Arsenal (2013)

Which English club has had the highest attendance of all time?

1	Man. City v Stoke	84,569	(1934)
2	Man. United v Arsenal	83,260	(1948)
3	Chelsea v Arsenal	82,905	(1935)
4	Everton v Liverpool	78,299	(1948)
5	Aston Villa v Derby	76,588	(1946)
6	Sunderland v Derby	75,118	(1933)
7	Tottenham v Sunderland	75,038	(1938)
8	Charlton v Aston Villa	75,031	(1938)
9	Arsenal v Lens	73,707	(1998)
10	Sheff. Wed. v Man. City	72,841	(1934)

Which club has won the most Champions Leagues?

1	Real Madrid	9 wins
2	AC Milan	7 wins
3	Liverpool	5 wins
	B. Munich	
5=	Barcelona	4 wins
	Ajax	
7=	Inter Milan	3 wins
	Man. United	
9=	Benfica	2 wins
	Juventus	
	Porto	
	Nott'm Forest	

Includes European Cup wins

Which country has provided the most Champions League winners?

1	Spain	13 wins
2=	Italy	12 wins
	England	
4	Germany	7 wins
5	Holland	6 wins
6	Portugal	4 wins
7=	France	1 win
	Scotland	
	Romania	
	Serbia/Yugoslavia	

Includes European Cup wins

Which team has won the most Spanish league titles?

1	Real Madrid	32
2	Barcelona	22
3	Atletico Madrid	9
4	Athletic Bilbao	8
5	Valencia	6
6	Real Sociedad	2
7=	Deportivo	1
	Sevilla	
	Real Betis	
10	n/a	

Which team has won the most Italian league titles?

1	Juventus	29*
2=	AC Milan	18
	Inter Milan	
4	Genoa	9
5=	Torino	7
	Bologna	
	Pro Vercelli	
8	Roma	3
9=	Lazio	2
	Napoli	
	Fiorentina	

*Juventus stripped of two titles

Which is the biggest stadium in Europe?

1	Nou Camp	Barcelona	99,354
2	Wembley	England	90,000
3	Bernabeu	Real Madrid	85,454
4	Signal Iduna Park	Borussia Dortmund	80,552
5	San Siro	Milan/Inter	80,074
6	Luzhniki Stadium	Spartak/CSKA Moscow	78,360
7	Ataturk Olympic Stadium	Istanbul BB	76,092
8	Old Trafford	Man. United	75,765
9	Millennium Stadium	Wales	74,500
10	Olympic Stadium	Hertha Berlin	74,220

Which current player has won the most international caps?

1	Ahmed Hassan	Egypt	184
2	Landon Donovan (pictured)	USA	151
3	Iker Casillas	Spain	149
4=	Gerardo Torrado	Mexico	144
	Salman Isa	Bahrain	
6	Anders Svensson	Sweden	142
7=	Yasuhito Endo	Japan	134
	Gianluigi Buffon	Italy	134
	Bader Al-Mutawa	Kuwait	134
10	Andres Oper	Estonia	133

Stats correct up to 31 August, 2013

Which team has won the most German league titles?

1	Bayern Munich	23
2	Nuremberg	9
3	Borussia Dortmund	8
4	Schalke	7
5	Hamburg	6
6=	Stuttgart	5
	B. Monchengladbach	
8=	Werder Bremen	4
	Kaiserslautern	
10=	Cologne	3
	Leipzig	
	SpVgg Furth	

Which European team has won their league the most?

1	Rangers (Scotland)	54 titles
2	Linfield (N. Ireland)	51 titles
3	Celtic (Scotland)	44 titles
4	Olympiakos (Greece)	40 titles
5=	Benfica (Portugal)	32 titles
	Rapid Vienna (Austria)	
	Real Madrid (Spain)	
	Ajax (Holland)	
	Anderlecht (Belgium)	
10	CSKA Sofia (Bulgaria)	31 titles

Which club makes the most money in a year?

1	Real Madrid	£445m
2	Barcelona	£418m
3	Man. United	£343m
4	Bayern Munich	£319m
5	Chelsea	£280m
6	Arsenal	£251m
7	Man. City	£248m
8	AC Milan	£222m
9	Liverpool	£202m
10	Juventus	£169m

Based on revenue for 2011-12 season

Which country has won the most World Cups?

1	Brazil	5 wins
2	Italy	4 wins
3	Germany	3 wins**
4=	Argentina	2 wins
	Uruguay	2 wins
6=	France	1 win
	England	1 win
	Spain	1 win
9	Holland	3 finals*
10	Czech Rep.	2 finals*

*Runners-up
**Includes victories under different names

Which country has won the most European Championships?

1=	Spain	3 wins
1=	Germany**	3 wins
3	France	2 wins
4=	Russia**	1 win
	Italy	1 win
	Czech Republic**	1 win
	Holland	1 win
	Denmark	1 win
	Greece	1 win
10	Serbia**	2 finals

*Runners-up
**Includes victories under different names

Who is England's most capped player of all time?

1	Peter Shilton	1970-1990	125 caps
2	David Beckham	1996-2009	115 caps
3	Bobby Moore	1962-1973	108 caps
4	Bobby Charlton	1958-1970	106 caps
5	Billy Wright	1946-1959	105 caps
6=	Ashley Cole	2001-	103 caps
	Steven Gerrard	2000-	103 caps
8	Frank Lampard	1999-	98 caps
9	Bryan Robson	1980-1991	90 caps
10	Michael Owen	1998-2008	89 caps

Stats correct up to 31 August, 2013

Paz & Bez's
TOP TENS

The 10 best keepers!

1	Manuel Neuer	Bayern Munich & Germany
2	Iker Casillas	Real Madrid & Spain
3	David De Gea	Man. United & Spain
4	Hugo Lloris	Tottenham & France
5	Gianluigi Buffon	Juventus & Italy
6	Joe Hart	Man. City & England
7	Petr Cech	Chelsea & Czech Republic
8	Thibaut Courtois	Atletico Madrid & Belgium
9	Salvatore Sirigu	PSG & Italy
10	Samir Handanovic	Inter Milan & Slovenia

The 10 best defenders!

1	Thiago Silva	PSG & Brazil
2	Philipp Lahm	Bayern Munich & Germany
3	Vincent Kompany	Man. City & Belgium
4	Mats Hummels	Borussia Dortmund & Germany
5	Dante	Bayern Munich & Brazil
6	Giorgio Chiellini	Juventus & Italy
7	Raphael Varane	Real Madrid & France
8	Andrea Barzagli	Juventus & Italy
9	Nemanja Vidic	Man. United & Serbia
10	David Alaba	Bayern Munich & Austria

The 10 best midfielders!

1	Andres Iniesta	Barcelona & Spain
2	Bastian Schweinsteiger	Bayern Munich & Germany
3	Xavi	Barcelona & Spain
4	Arturo Vidal	Juventus & Chile
5	Andrea Pirlo	Juventus & Italy
6	Mesut Ozil	Arsenal & Germany
7	Javi Martinez	Bayern Munich & Spain
8	Toni Kroos	Bayern Munich & Germany
9	Juan Mata	Chelsea & Spain
10	Yaya Toure	Man. City & Ivory Coast

The 10 best forwards!

1	Lionel Messi	Barcelona & Argentina
2	Cristiano Ronaldo	Real Madrid & Portugal
3	Gareth Bale	Real Madrid & Wales
4	Radamel Falcao	Monaco & Colombia
5	Robin Van Persie	Man. United & Holland
6	Robert Lewandowski	Borussia Dortmund & Poland
7	Luis Suarez	Liverpool & Uruguay
8	Neymar	Barcelona & Brazil
9	Zlatan Ibrahimovic	PSG & Sweden
10	Edinson Cavani	PSG & Uruguay

NOW IT'S YOUR TURN!

MY TOP 10 Players in the world!

1	Messi	6	Zlatan
2	Ronaldo	7	Hazard
3	Neur	8	Bale
4	Neymar	9	Silva
5	Suarez	10	Lahm

IS THAT REALLY LINEKER?

When we saw this pic of Gary Lineker from the 1980s, it got us thinking: what if today's stars had been playing 30 years ago – what would THEY have looked like?

CHELSEA

Frank LAMPARD

LIVERPOOL

Steven GERRARD

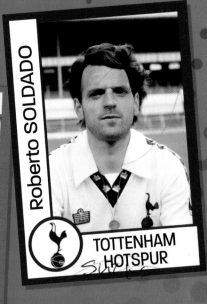

Roberto SOLDADO

TOTTENHAM HOTSPUR

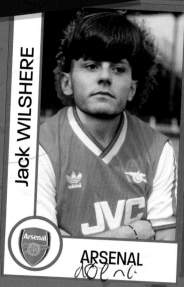

Jack WILSHERE

ARSENAL

ENGLAND

Joe HART

MAN. UNITED

Rio FERDINAND

EICESTER

Gary LINEKER

ARSENAL

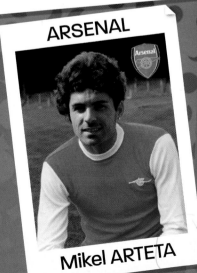

Mikel ARTETA

MAN. UNITED

Michael CARRICK

Monkey business!

Stephan El Shaarawy's fan club wait for their hero at AC Milan's training ground!

Andre Villas-Boas was shocked to see his long-lost brother turn up at White Hart Lane!

Tong the chimp is crowned winner of the 2013 Pull A Phil Jones Face competition!

Liverpool fan Chippy the chimp hears the news that Sir Alex Ferguson has retired as Man. United boss!

TIME FOR A SPACE HUNT!

10 THINGS FOR YOU TO FIND...

NEYMAR

FIDO THE SPACE DOG

THE WORLD CUP TROPHY

CLIVE THE CYCLOPS

WAZMAN AND ROBIN

SUPER-BALE

MISTER SLIMY

GLOBBO THE MARTIAN KING

HOWARD WEBB

CRISTIANO RONALDO

STEVEN GERRARD
ENGLAND

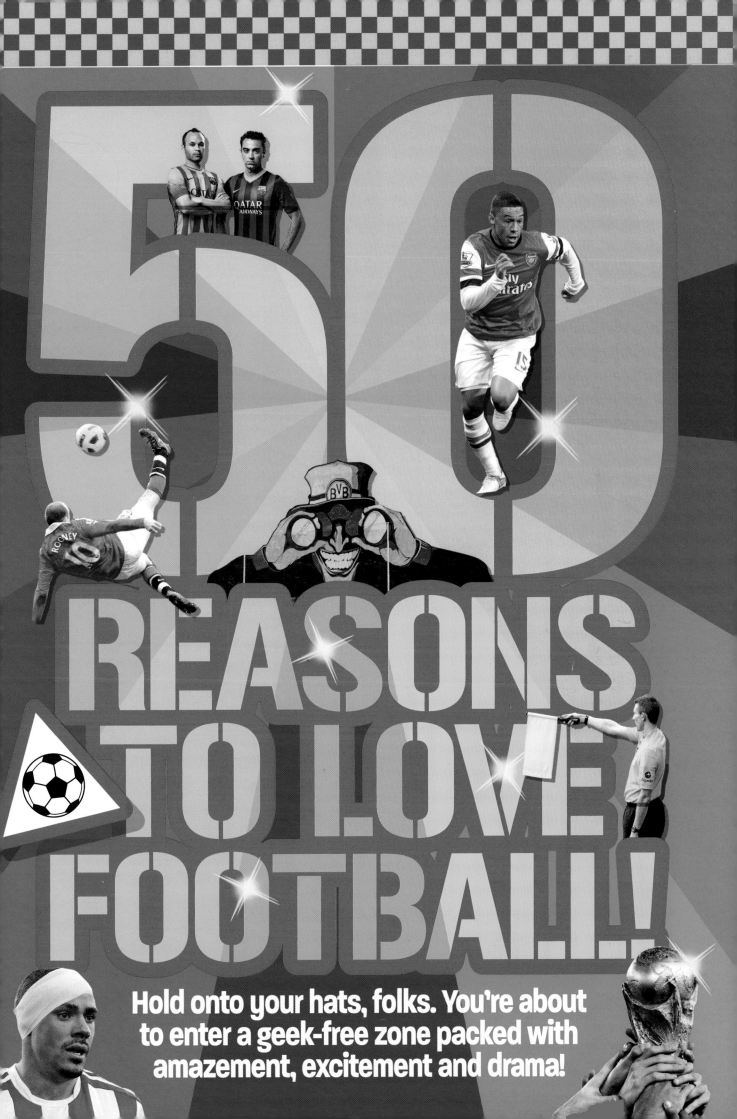

50 REASONS TO LOVE FOOTBALL!

Hold onto your hats, folks. You're about to enter a geek-free zone packed with amazement, excitement and drama!

50

WINGERS!
How can you not love a bit of turbo-charged wizardry on the wing!

49

46

HEAD BANDAGES!
No-one likes a clash of heads. But everyone loves a daft player wrapped up like an Egyptian mummy!

47

WATERLOGGED PITCHES!
Splish, splosh, splash – it's time to unpack the snorkel!

BRAGA'S STADIUM!
Apart from having a Brazilian winger called Alan, the best thing about the Portuguese club is their ridiculous stadium. Yep, it's in a mountain!

HOLLAND FANS!
In Holland you can only buy orange clothes. Look, it's true!

48

EVENING MATCHES!
Footy under the moon and the fuzzy glow of floodlights rocks!

45

WEMBLEY STADIUM!
Yeah, we know it cost about a gazillion pounds but it's one giant football bowl of atmosphere, memories and brilliance!

44

43

REFS FALLING OVER!
It's the same as seeing one of your teachers take a tumble in the playground. Pure comedy gold!

ONE-TWOS!
If you can't go through them, go round them with a cheeky little one-two!

42

▶▶▶ **TURN OVER FOR MORE!**

41 PLAYING IN SNOW!
Only one rule: don't use the white ball!

40 DISALLOWED GOALS!
When the opposition fans are already celebrating a goal, there's nothing quite like the peep of the whistle and the sight of the lino's raised flag to shut them up!

39

BACKHEELS!
You know when you pretend to throw a ball for a dog, but don't really throw it, and the clueless mutt goes bounding off into the distance in a state of confusion. A backheel does that to a defender!

33 THE FA CUP!
Don't believe in the magic of the FA Cup? Then go to the doctors, pronto, as there's something wrong with you!

32 LA LIGA!
There's nothing like settling down in front of the TV on a Sunday night to watch Real Madrid give a team full of Spanish chumps a real good thrashing!

38

GOAL-LINE CLEARANCES!
Oh no, they've scored! The opposition fans are cheering, the striker is celebrating. But, hang on, incredibly, a random leg hooks it off the line!

37

CUP UPSETS!
Big club + banana skin + a hairy underdog + the TV cameras = a giant upset + mega lolz!

36

NUTMEGS!
How to embarrass and annoy someone in one not-so-easy, awesome move!

35

OUTFIELD PLAYERS GOING IN GOAL!
You've used all your subs and your keeper gets sent off – there's only one solution. It's time for one of your outfielders to don the sweaty Sondicos!

34

FOREIGN FANS!
They're kerr-razy!

31

FINGERTIP SAVES!
Keepers can be match-winners too – by pulling off a gravity-defying, acrobatic stop!

▶▶▶ **TURN OVER FOR MORE!**

COMEDY OWN GOALS!

Defenders have got one job – and that's to stop the opposition from scoring. So at what point did it seem like a good idea to score for them yourself, ya flamin' galah?

30

28

STEP-OVERS!

He's gonna go one way but he goes the other. It's one for the tricksters!

29

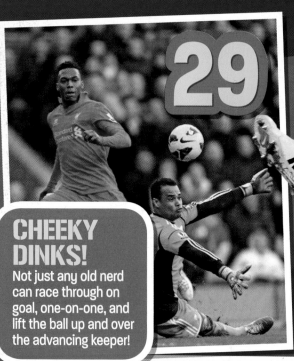

CHEEKY DINKS!

Not just any old nerd can race through on goal, one-on-one, and lift the ball up and over the advancing keeper!

24

BULLET HEADERS!

A fizzed-in cross met with the forehead of a goal-hungry striker is as English as fish and chips! Salt and vinegar? Yes, please!

23

THE PREMIER LEAGUE!

There's a reason the Prem is watched all over the world – and it's not for Big Sam's face. It's for the excitement, the goals, the drama and the atmosphere!

BARCELONA 2009-13!

Football was invented in the 1800s – that's like a million years ago – and yet you are lucky enough to be alive at the same time as THE BEST TEAM THAT'S EVER PLAYED THE GAME!

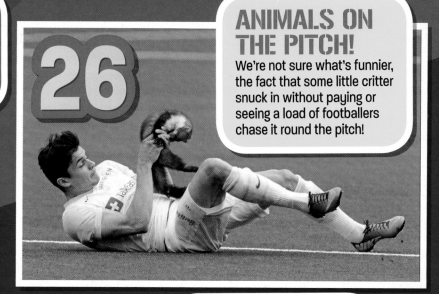

ANIMALS ON THE PITCH!

We're not sure what's funnier, the fact that some little critter snuck in without paying or seeing a load of footballers chase it round the pitch!

THE EUROS!

Europe's best 24 nations, together, in one tournament, for one month, every four years – come on, that's pretty special!

FINAL-DAY DECIDERS!

A whole season coming down to 90 nerve-jangling minutes. Take some deep breaths – it's gonna be a bumpy ride!

TRANSFER DEADLINE DAY!

When else would you get excited about a Bulgarian being spotted on the M6 or a 33-year-old Russian arriving at Stansted Airport?

▶▶▶ TURN OVER FOR MORE!

20

RABONA!

Not the drink made from the blood of Ribena berries – we're talking about the round-the-back-of-the-leg flick that only the top flair players can pull off!

15

THE CHAMPIONS LEAGUE MUSIC!

The players walk out onto the pitch, the violins start, then the operatic singing kicks in, the music gets louder, the singing gets louder, and then – hum, hum, hum THE CHAMPIONS. Goosebumps time!

UEFA CHAMPIONS LEAGUE   FINAL WEMBLEY 2013

14

XAVI & INIESTA!

The greatest double act since MOTD's Paz & Bez!

19

FLARES!

Like smoke? Like colour? Then you'll love a flare! Generally found doing their thing in South American stadiums!

17

DIVING HEADERS!

This isn't a swimming pool, son. We'll have no diving here – oh, unless it's a bloomin' beautiful header!

18

PANENKA!

Those penalties where the taker runs up to the ball and just when you think they're going to smash it, they casually dink it right down the middle, making the keeper look like a right mug!

16

KEEPERS GOING UP FOR CORNERS!

What's that clown doing up there? He's not thinking of getting his head on this, is he? Wait a minute – oh my word, GOAL!

13

THE BOMBONERA!

The home of Argentinian club Boca Juniors and 49,000 loony supporters!

12

THUMPING VOLLEYS!

Bosh! Crashing a volley past a despairing keeper is the main reason humans have feet!

▶▶▶ TURN OVER FOR MORE!

11

FREE-KICKS INTO THE TOP CORNER FROM 30 YARDS!

Commentator: "It looks like he's going for goal, Andy!"

Co-commentator: "Well, that's stupid, Clive. He must be, what, 30 yards from goal!"

Commentator: "Ha! And some! But he is you know. Here he comes!"

Co-commentator: "Oh, he's struck that well, lifted it up over the wall!"

Commentator: "Gooooooaaaaal!"

Co-commentator: "I told you, Clive. That's what he's capable of!"

06

PENALTY SAVES!

The moment a keeper becomes a hero!

09

LONG-RANGE SCREAMERS!

He's not gonna shoot from there is he? He is, you know! Boom – what a goal!

05

PENALTY SHOOT-OUTS!

The drama, the tension, the nerves. For the winners, a moment of ecstasy, for the losers, a lifetime of regret. And tears – always tears!

10

COMEBACKS!

The magical feeling of coming from 2-0 down to win 3-2 will lodge itself in your memory forever!

CRISTIANO RONALDO!

For moments of awesomeness, you can't outgun C-Ron. Describe him in one word? Okay, how about: BEAST!

07

08

SHOTS GOING IN OFF THE UNDERSIDE OF THE BAR!

Any long distance strike is automatically improved 100% if it thumps the underside of the bar, bounces down and then back up into the roof of the net!

04

BICYCLE KICKS!

Executing an overhead kick and seeing the ball hit the back of the net is the moment you feel like saying: "You know what? My life is not going to get any better than this. I retire!"

▶▶▶ **TURN OVER FOR MORE!**

03

THE WORLD CUP!
The best month of your life – it really is as simple as that!

02

LIONEL MESSI!
When you're 80 years old, sat in your comfy chair with a pocket of 2ps and a few stray Polos, you can tell your grandkids that YOU saw Lionel Messi play – YOU saw the greatest player of all time!

01

LAST-MINUTE WINNERS!

Yes, yes, yes, yes, yes! Get in there! You beauty! Nothing, we repeat, nothing, is better than netting a dramatic, spine-tingling last-minute winner. Yesssss!

CROSSWORD!

Forget those boring crosswords OAPs do, here's a special footy one just for you!

5 POINTS for each right answer!

3 MALAYA

2 BENWAT

4 BENWAT

ACROSS

1 Northampton's nickname (8)

2 Man. United manager (5, 5)

3 Santi Cazorla joined Arsenal from this club (6)

4 2010 World Cup hosts (5, 6)

5 Scored the winner in this year's FA Cup Final (3, 6)

DOWN

1 Monaco striker Radamel Falcao plays for this country (8)

2 Last season's top scorer in the Premier League (5, 3, 6)

3 Mesut Ozil joined Arsenal from this Spanish club (4, 6)

4 Galatasaray's country (6)

5 Europa League champions (7)

6 Name of Barcelona's stadium (3, 4)

7 The club from Carrow Road (7)

MY SCORE ☐ OUT OF 60

ANSWERS ON p92

TURN TO p72 FOR MORE QUIZ ACTION!

Can you win...
THE PREMIER

HOW TO PLAY
Grab some mates and a dice. Take it in turns to roll the dice and move along the squares. If you land on a red square, do what it tells you. The first player to reach the finish is the winner!

START!

You string together a six-game winning streak. Move forward five spaces!

Your new wonderkid scores on his debut. Move forward four spaces!

Your chairman sells your star playmaker to Barcelona. Move back 11 spaces!

You sign a top-class striker on deadline day. Move forward nine spaces!

Two of your star players have a huge training ground bust-up. Move back five spaces!

Your title rivals' No.1 keeper dislocates his shoulder. Move forward six spaces!

Eight first-teamers are struck down by a stomach bug. Move back five spaces!

1 2 3 4 5 6 7 8

33 34 35 36 37 38 39 40

41 42 43 44 45 46 47 48 49 50

51 52 53 54 55 56 57 58

59 60 61 62 63 64 65 66 67

LEAGUE?

Have you got what it takes to be crowned Prem champions?

Your left-back's last-minute own goal means you lose your local derby. **Move back four spaces!**

Your keeper's 90th-minute penalty save secures three vital points. **Move forward three spaces!**

Your top scorer breaks his leg and is out for the season. **Move back 15 spaces!**

Your assistant quits to become boss of a Championship club. **Move back five spaces!**

You beat your title rivals 3-2 in a crucial six-pointer. **Move forward five spaces!**

FINISH!
The fans are going wild for the new Prem champions!

MATCH OF THE DAY

10 11 12 13 14 15 16 17 18 19 20 21 22 23 24 25 26 27 28 29 30 31 32 68 69 70 71 72 73 74 75

STAT★ATTACK DAVID BECKHAM!

His amazing career in stats!

1992-2013	719 GAMES	129 GOALS

115
He has 115 England caps – a record for an outfield player!

17
Becks scored 17 goals for England!

He is the only Englishman to score at three World Cups!

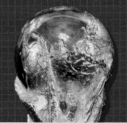

v Colombia, 1998

v Argentina, 2002

v Ecuador, 2006

MAN. UNITED
394 Games
85 Goals

PRESTON
5 Games
2 Goals

REAL MADRID
155 Games
20 Goals

LA GALAXY
118 Games
20 Goals

AC MILAN
33 Games
2 Goals

PSG
14 Games
0 Goals

9

Becks was sent off nine times in his career!

107

He played 107 Champions League games – and was the first Englishman to play in more than 100!

Beckham won league titles in

FOUR

different countries – England, Spain, USA and France!

10 million

The number of Beckham shirts sold throughout his career!

58%

of his Premier League goals for Man. United were scored from outside the area!

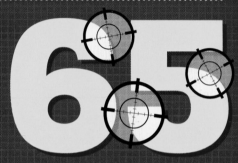

65

He scored an incredible 65 free-kicks in his career!

28m

people have liked his Facebook page!

137 million

The number of results you get when you search for Beckham's name on Google!

*All stats correct up to August 2013

MAN. UNITED
Premier League champions 2012-13

WORLD CUP BRAZIL 2014

MOTD looks ahead to next summer's World Cup, so strap yourself in – it's gonna be Braziliant!

5 THINGS YOU NEED TO KNOW!

5
It all kicks off on 12 June!

4
It'll be the 20th World Cup!

3
32 teams compete over 32 days!

2
12 epic stadiums will be used!

1
There can only be 1 winner!

5 TEAMS YOU SHOULD FEAR!

1 SPAIN
Reigning champions and still going strong!
Star man: Andres Iniesta

2 ARGENTINA
Won it last time it was held in South America!
Star man: Lionel Messi

3 GERMANY
Players are doing the business at club level!
Star man: Bastian Schweinsteiger

60 SECOND GUIDE TO BRAZIL!

The facts!
Capital: Brasilia
Language: Portuguese
Population: 194 million
Area: 8,515,767 km2
Currency: Real (R$)

BRAZIL

RAINFOREST
More than half of the Amazon rainforest is located in Brazil!

RIO DE JANEIRO
Home of Christ The Redeemer, the Maracana Stadium and the Copacabana beach. Wicked!

SAO PAULO
With 11m people, it's the largest city in Brazil!

4 BRAZIL
Home advantage means they're serious contenders this time!
Star man: Neymar

5 BELGIUM
Their young crop of exciting stars could stun the footy world!
Star man: Eden Hazard

ROY HODGSON'S GUIDE TO... BRAZILIAN ANIMALS!

ROY SAYS: "This lil' blighter is a baby elephant zebra!"
No, Roy, it's a Brazilian tapir!

ROY SAYS: "This critter is a manky fish monkey!"
No, Roy, it's a two-toed sloth!

ROY SAYS: "This must be a Simonus Cowellus chimp!"
No, it's a brown capuchin!

ROY SAYS: "This crazy fella is a trunk-nosed squirter!"
No, Roy, it's a giant anteater!

ROY SAYS: "This is a dog!"
No, Roy, it's an armadillo!

60 SECOND GUIDE TO THE WORLD CUP!

The last World Cup!

When: 2010
Where: South Africa
Winners: Spain
Top scorer: Thomas Muller, Germany – 5
Player Of The Tournament: Diego Forlan, Uruguay

World Cup history!

The first World Cup was held in Uruguay in 1930. The hosts beat Argentina in the final!

Brazil have qualified for and won more tournaments than any other country!

England won the tournament in 1966 and reached the semi-final in 1990!

That's how you do it, Roy!

MOTD STAT:
Spain won the last World Cup and the past TWO European Championships!

5 WORLD CUP LEGENDS!

1954
Just Fontaine
France

1970
Pele
Brazil

1986
Maradona
Argentina

1998
Zinedine Zidane
France

2002
Ronaldo
Brazil

WORLD CUP QUIZ TIME!

1 What was the score in the 2010 World Cup Final?

2 Who was top scorer at the 1986 World Cup in Mexico?

3 Why did this dog become a celebrity in 1966?

4 Which team knocked England out in 1986 and 1998?

5 Where was the 2006 tournament held?

ANSWERS
1 Spain 1-0 Holland, 2 Gary Lineker, 3 Pickles the dog, found the World Cup trophy, which had been stolen, 4 Argentina 5 Germany

RADAMEL FALCAO
COLOMBIA

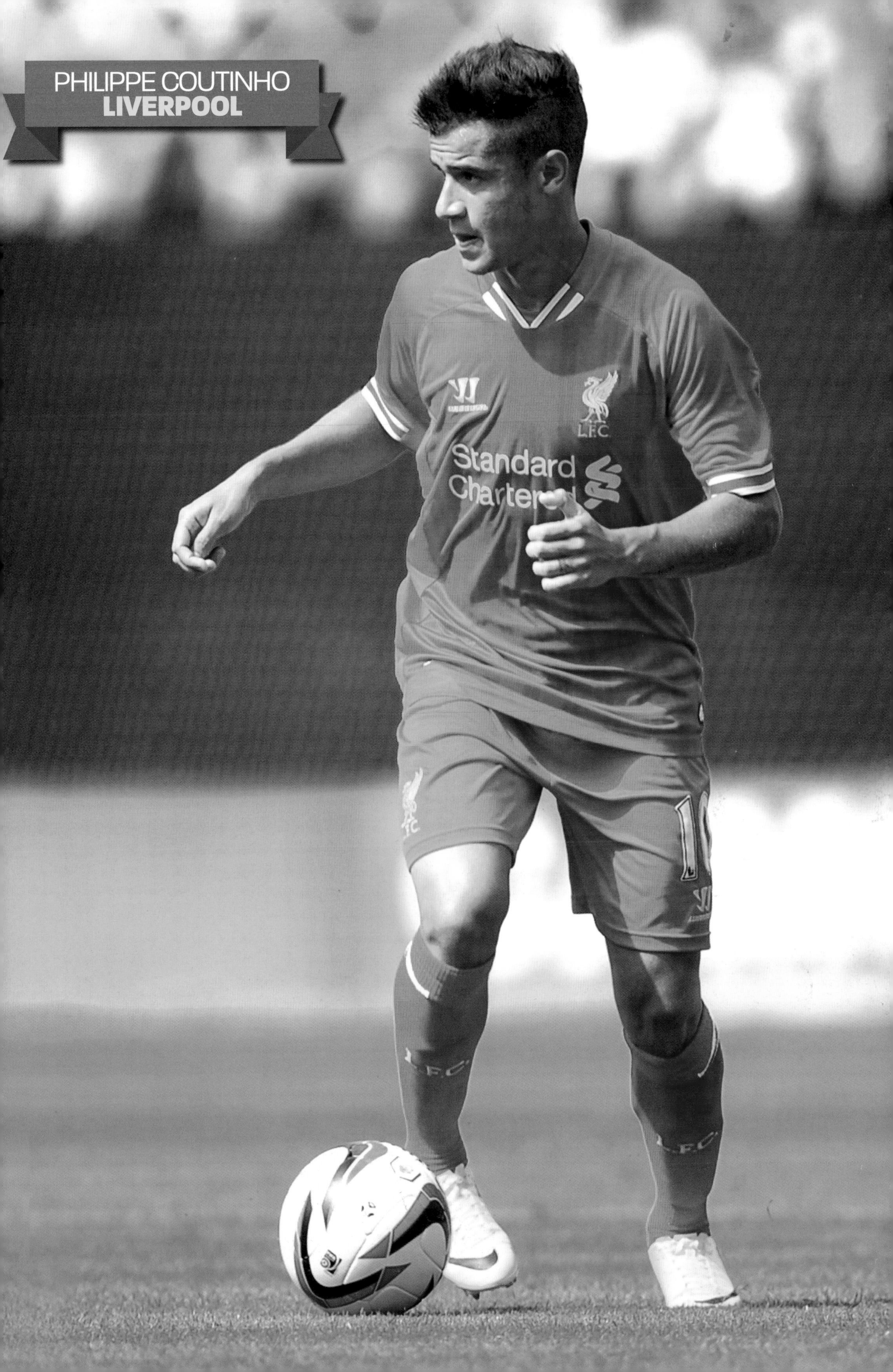
PHILIPPE COUTINHO
LIVERPOOL

THE HOT

MOTD's big two go head-to-head and tackle footy's hottest topics!

Who is your favourite player?	Who is the best team in the world?	Who will be the star of 2014?

The presenter
Name: Gary Lineker
Clubs: Leicester, Everton, Barcelona, Tottenham, Nagoya Grampus Eight
England games/goals: 80/48
Club games/goals: 568/281

Lineker says: "Lionel Messi – he's just a phenomenon and so very talented. He just defies belief and is breaking every record that ever existed. He really is incredible!"

Lineker says: "Well, Bayern Munich were last season. However, that changes all the time. People work out how to play against teams – you saw that happen with Barcelona!"

Lineker says: "I think Messi will be the star – but it'll be really interesting to see how Neymar does at Barcelona. There's also Ronaldo, obviously, as well as Gareth Bale!"

The pundit
Name: Alan Shearer
Clubs: Southampton, Blackburn, Newcastle
England games/goals: 63/30
Club games/goals: 733/379

Shearer says: "Lionel Messi. He can score every type of goal, he scores almost every game and he plays like he's a kid having a kickabout in the park. Nothing bothers him!"

Shearer says: "Bayern. They've been in three of the last four Champions League finals. They finally got the win they deserved last season!"

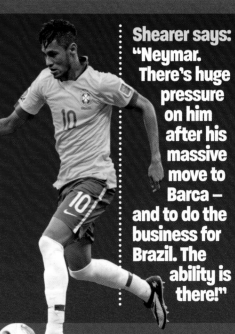

Shearer says: "Neymar. There's huge pressure on him after his massive move to Barca – and to do the business for Brazil. The ability is there!"

SEAT!

WITH GARY LINEKER & ALAN SHEARER!

Who will win the World Cup?	What is the best stadium in the world?	What's the best moment of your career?	Where is the best place to go on holiday?	Who'd win in an MOTD arm wrestle?
Lineker says: "History tells us that if the World Cup is held in South America, a South American team wins it. Because of that, and the brilliance of Messi, Argentina!"	**Lineker says:** "Wembley and the Allianz are great. The Nou Camp is a brilliant place to play – it looks a bit tired now. It's the same as when I was there 25 years ago!"	**Lineker says:** "Winning the Golden Boot at the 1986 World Cup in Mexico. It changed my life!" 	**Lineker says:** "Barcelona is my favourite city in the world. But I also love to go and visit places like Italy, Los Angeles and Paris – LA is more like a second home for me now!"	**Lineker says:** "I work out quite a lot and I'm pretty darn strong. But, let's put it this way, Lawrenson and Hansen wouldn't have a chance. It would be a Shearer v Lineker final!"
Shearer says: "Spain will be favourites but it'll be fascinating. Brazil are a big danger playing in front of their home fans, so their hopes should not be taken lightly!"	**Shearer says:** "Wembley is superb. It's a very special place. The atmosphere in the old stadium was even better than the new one. I was lucky enough to play there!"	**Shearer says:** "The day I was named captain of England!" 	**Shearer says:** "Barbados! I love the culture, the weather, the people and the amazing atmosphere over there. The beach and the restaurants really are excellent!"	**Shearer says:** "I'm by far the youngest, so I'd be gutted if I didn't win!" 

I spy with my little eye LITTLE RON!

That little chap in his ill-fitting blue tracksuit and rascal red shoes may look like any badly dressed toddler from the late 1980s but it's not – it's global megastar Cristiano Ronaldo. It's safe to say that Portugal ace C-Ron has upped his game in the fashion stakes over the past 25 years. But we want him to bring back the afro!

From tracksuit in 1988 – to black suit in 2013!

Dude, that haircut stinks!

SESAME STREET
The Prem is full of Muppets!
Which footballers could replace their fluffy TV lookalikes?

Marouane Fellaini as Big Bird

Dimitar Berbatov as The Count

David Silva as Grover

THE £1 BILLION
DREAM TEAM!

This epic all-star line-up brings together stars from all over the globe with the biggest price tags in their position!

THIAGO SILVA

NEUER

KOMPANY

ALABA

LAHM

SCHWEINSTEIGER

WILSHERE

INIESTA

RONALDO

BALE

MESSI

Total value:
£935m

KEEPER!
MANUEL NEUER
BAYERN MUNICH

Gianluigi Buffon is the most expensive keeper of all time after moving for £32 million 12 years ago – but any team wishing to get their hands on this 27-year-old will have to smash that transfer record to smithereens!

Transfer value:
£60m

RIGHT-BACK!
PHILIPP LAHM
BAYERN MUNICH

Full-backs are criminally under-rated – and Philipp Lahm might just be the most under-rated player ever. You see, he NEVER puts a foot wrong. And so even though he's 29, Bayern would need a massive offer to consider selling!

Transfer value:
£35m

Transfer value:
£40m

LEFT-BACK!
DAVID ALABA
BAYERN MUNICH

Introducing the ultimate modern full-back – Alaba's super-quick, attack-minded and great on the ball. At 21, he's got a decade at the top ahead of him and that's why the Austrian superstar is going to cost big bucks!

CENTRE-BACK!

THIAGO SILVA
PSG

This 28-year-old Brazilian moves around the pitch like he's strolling down Copacabana beach on a balmy summer's evening. He never breaks a sweat, he's always in the right place at the right time and is the world's best centre-back!

Transfer value:
£50m

Transfer value:
£50m

CENTRE-BACK!

VINCENT KOMPANY MAN. CITY

When you're ticking off the skills you want in a captain and centre-back, you realise Vinny has got them all. He's 27, reaching his peak and is the man you want to build your defence around. And that doesn't come cheap!

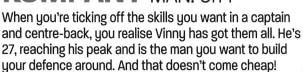

MIDFIELDER!

BASTIAN SCHWEINSTEIGER
BAYERN MUNICH

Quite simply a machine in the middle of the park. He's not fancy, he's not a showman, but he is the best in the world at combining brains and brawn – out-muscling opponents, keeping possession and driving Bayern Munich forward!

Transfer value:
£60m

MIDFIELDER!

JACK WILSHERE
ARSENAL

The only English player who could walk into any team in the world. He's been troubled by injuries but when he's fit, his explosive bursts forward can change the flow of a game – making him a much-wanted midfield megastar!

Transfer value:
£60m

MIDFIELDER!

ANDRES INIESTA
BARCELONA

You can't put a price on magic, and that's what this Spanish midfield magician provides in abundance. The only reason he's not worth £100 million is that at 29, he's only got five years left in his little legs – but it'll be a glorious five years!

Transfer value:
£80m

FORWARD!

CRISTIANO RONALDO
REAL MADRID

C-Ron's £80 million move to Real four years ago makes him the most expensive player in the history of football, but he's worth even more now. He scores more goals than he plays games. That's insane and so is his enormous price tag!

Transfer value:
£150m

FORWARD!

GARETH BALE
REAL MADRID

Match-winners don't come cheap. You won't find them in the bargain basket of your local supermarket and you're not going to buy one and get one free. That's why Bale is now one of the most valuable players on the planet – coz he's a grade A match-winner!

Transfer value:
£100m

FORWARD!

LIONEL MESSI
BARCELONA

We all know there's more chance of a dog becoming Prime Minister than Messi leaving his beloved Barcelona – but a mega bid of £250 million would be enough to secure the services of the little Argentinian wizard. That's right, 250 million big ones – wow!

I am your new Prime Minister!

Transfer value:
£250m

ALL-TIME MOST EXPENSIVE TEAM!

So that's the most expensive team if you were buying them today – but what is the most expensive team of all time based on actual transfers that have happened?

GIANLUIGI BUFFON
PARMA TO JUVENTUS
£32m

DANI ALVES
SEVILLA TO BARCELONA
£28m

THIAGO SILVA
AC MILAN TO PSG
£36m

RIO FERDINAND
LEEDS TO MAN. UNITED
£30m

FABIO COENTRAO
BENFICA TO REAL MADRID
£26m

KAKA
AC MILAN TO REAL MADRID
£56m

GARETH BALE
TOTTENHAM TO REAL MADRID
£85m

CRISTIANO RONALDO
MAN. UNITED TO REAL MADRID
£80m

NEYMAR
SANTOS TO BARCELONA
£51m

EDINSON CAVANI
NAPOLI TO PSG
£55m

ZLATAN IBRAHIMOVIC
INTER MILAN TO BARCELONA
£59m

Total value:
£538m

Footy map of EUROPE!

- Stuck in an ice age!
- Zlatan & 10 others!
- Home of bears Arshavin and Abramovich!
- The Tartan Army!
- Norn Iron!
- Long-ball merchants!
- Team Keano!
- 1966 World Cup winners!
- RVP!
- Great players – rubbish music!
- Lewandowski & pals!
- Should stick to ice hockey!
- Gareth Bale!
- Dark horses!
- Famous for Euro 2012 and chicken Kievs!
- Ooh la la – they're falling out again!
- Toblerone munchers!
- Republic of Modric!
- Rubbish at football!
- Good in the 1990s!
- Born to defend – and use hair gel!
- Vidic-ville!
- Berbatov empire!
- Not fans of Lionel Messi!
- Pass teams to death!
- Dzeko-land!
- Crazy fa[n]
- Tongue-twisting surnames!

---

5 STUPID CLUB BADGES! (and they're all real)

Club: Bari
Country: Italy
What is it? A terrified version of the famous Corn Flakes chicken!

Club: Avenir Beggen
Country: Luxembourg
What is it? A bearded elf wearing a witch's hat sitting on a ball!

Club: Gombak United
Country: Singapore
What is it? A weird bull keeper with a red cone on his bonce!

Club: Cologne
Country: Germany
What is it? A goat so bored that he's trying to climb the badge!

Club: Thanh Hoa
Country: Vietnam
What is it? A big ball, a blue bridge, hills and a warrior on a horse!

PENALTY SHOOT-OUT GAME

Can you handle the pressure?

HOW TO PLAY!
Grab a dice or download a dice app. Take it in turns to roll the dice – the number it lands on decides where your penalty goes. Repeat this for all five pens and the player with the most successful spot kicks is the winner!

Are you deadly from 12 yards or will you crumble? It's time for the most nerve-wracking thing in footy – the dreaded penalty shoot-out!

THE SCOREBOARD

Record your results here! ✓ = Goal ✗ = Miss

NAME	PEN 1	PEN 2	PEN 3	PEN 4	PEN 5	NAME	PEN 1	PEN 2	PEN 3	PEN 4	PEN 5
Cristiano	✗	✗	✗	✓	✓	rangers	✓	✗	✗	✗	✗
Barca	✓	✗	✓	✗	✓	realm	✗	✗	✗	✓	✓
adv	✗	✗	✗	✗	✓	bay	✗	✗	✗	✓	✓

PAZ & BEZ'S FOOTY FACTS!

100% TRUE!

1
Growing up was a hoot for Roy!

Roy Hodgson was raised by owls in a barn in Shropshire!

2
Neymar's polar express!

Brazilian superstar Neymar travels to matches on the back of an orphaned polar bear whose name is Norman!

3
Sneezy does it!

Swansea star Michu was meant to be called Mitch, but his mum sneezed while confirming his name to person filling out his birth certificate!

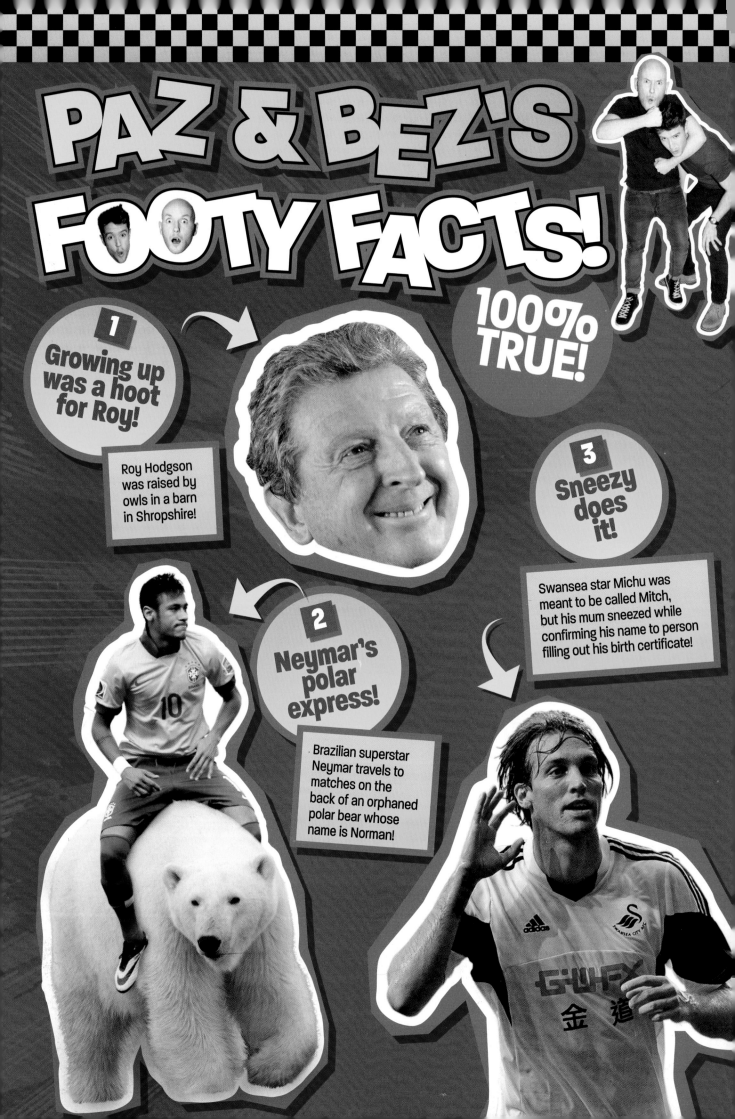

4 Lennon's food for thought!

Aaron Lennon lives exclusively on a diet of alphabetti spaghetti!

HEINZ alphabetti
pasta in our classic tomato sauce
LOVE ...the taste!

5 Chores and snores!

As a youngster Wayne Rooney would switch on a vacuum cleaner before going to bed, claiming the roaring noise helped him get to sleep!

6 No rest for the wicked!

Newcastle's midfield hardman Cheick Tiote hasn't slept for six years – he says sleeping is for wimps!

7 Toure family affair!

Man. City midfielder Yaya Toure has a brother called Kolo, a sister called Yolo, a cousin called Rolo, an uncle called Polo, an aunt called Zolo and a dog called Dave!

Okay, only one is true – but can you guess which one!

ANSWER: The true fact is No.6 – Wayne Rooney used to sleep with the vacuum cleaner on. Ha!

PAZ or BEZ WHO ARE YOU?

Which of our dynamic duo are you most like?

It's Saturday afternoon – what are you up to?
A Watching an action-packed Football League match!
B Enjoying some world-class footy at a swanky Premier League stadium!
C Chewing a clump of grass before having a nap!

You find a stray £5 note – what do you do?
A Buy some Haribo, Nice 'n' Spicy Nik Naks and a bottle of cherry Coke!
B Buy some Minstrels, chocolate biscuits and a bottle of Diet Coke!
C Eat it!

You're playing 5-a-side – what are you doing?
A Playing cheeky, one-touch passes – there's no need to run around like a headless chicken!
B Winning the ball back straight away and setting off on a mazy dribble!
C Chomping on a discarded Mars Bar!

You're getting ready to go out – what are you doing with your hair?
A Erm, hair, you say? Erm, how about some moisturiser?
B It's all about the bounce – so a load of mousse, blow dry and repeat!
C Trying to lick the fleas out of it!

Mostly As	Mostly Bs	Mostly Cs
You're Paz!	You're Bez!	You're a llama!

MATCH OF THE DAY KICKABOUT

Catch Paz & Bez on **MOTD Kickabout** CBBC, Saturday mornings!

Who are ya?

This one is simple – how many of the 20 Premier
League players pictured below can you name?

2 POINTS for each right answer!

1 Evans

2 Coleman

3 Olsson

4 Answer

5 Answer

6 Answer

7 Answer

8 Answer

9 Answer

10 Answer

11 Answer

12 Answer

13 Answer

14 Answer

15 Answer

16 Answer

17 Answer

18 Answer

19 Answer

20 Answer

MY SCORE ☐ OUT OF **40**

ANSWERS ON p92

TURN TO p82 FOR MORE QUIZ ACTION!

LUIS SUAREZ
URUGUAY

FUTURE OF FOOTBALL!

We count down the stars fighting to be the next big thing!

15 RUBEN LOFTUS-CHEEK

Tall and elegant box-to-box midfielder who dominates the opposition!

FACTBOX

CLUB:
Chelsea

COUNTRY:
England

BORN:
Lewisham, England

AGE:
17

POSITION:
Midfielder

DID YOU KNOW?
Ruben has captained England Schoolboys in the Victory Shield!

POTENTIAL VALUE!
£25 MILLION

PLAYING STYLE : You get some midfielders blessed with creativity and some are natural-born tacklers – but on rare occasions a player comes along who can do everything. Say hello to Ruben Loftus-Cheek, two class midfielders in one!

14 MATIJA NASTASIC

Composed centre-back who's a master at tackling and reading the game!

FACTBOX

CLUB:
Man. City

COUNTRY:
Serbia

BORN:
Valjevo, Serbia

AGE:
20

POSITION:
Centre-back

DID YOU KNOW? Nastasic is good friends with city rival Nemanja Vidic!

POTENTIAL VALUE!
£26 MILLION

PLAYING STYLE: Centre-backs peak towards their late twenties, so the fact that this Serbian cruncher was playing for the Prem champs when he was still a teenager tells you all you need to know. He's special and is getting better!

13 WILFRIED ZAHA

Dazzling trickster with explosive acceleration and bags of confidence!

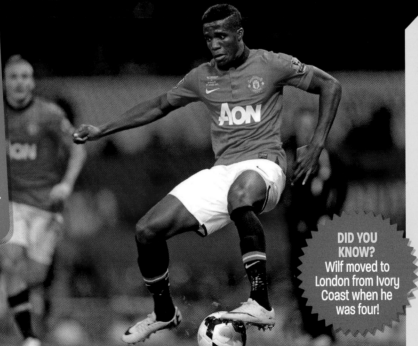

FACTBOX

CLUB:
Man. United

COUNTRY:
England

BORN:
Abidjan, Ivory Coast

AGE:
20

POSITION:
Winger

DID YOU KNOW? Wilf moved to London from Ivory Coast when he was four!

POTENTIAL VALUE!
£28 MILLION

PLAYING STYLE: A wriggling, slippery, nut-megging nightmare for full-backs. He'll be surrounded by defenders, but then, in the blink of an eye, pull out some extravagant stepover combo and race into the box. Textbook Zaha!

12 RAHEEM STERLING

Jet-heeled winger with blistering pace and excellent dribbling ability!

FACTBOX

CLUB:
Liverpool

COUNTRY:
England

BORN:
Kingston, Jamaica

AGE:
18

POSITION:
Winger

POTENTIAL VALUE!
£28 MILLION

DID YOU KNOW? Sterling once scored five in one game for Liverpool's youth team!

PLAYING STYLE
If you read any wildlife book, it'll tell you that cheetahs are the fastest mammals on earth. Yeah, well that was before Raheem was born – because this kid is pure pace. His darting runs leave defenders in a spin!

---

11 ADNAN JANUZAJ

Cool and composed Belgian unlocks defences with cheeky passes!

FACTBOX

CLUB:
Man. United

COUNTRY:
Belgium

BORN:
Brussels, Belgium

AGE:
18

POSITION:
Midfielder

POTENTIAL VALUE!
£30 MILLION

DID YOU KNOW? He was United reserves' player Of The Year last season!

PLAYING STYLE
The Belgian football conveyer belt has turned out another future star here. Adnan's one of those players who gets pundits purring – he's got the silky first touch, the superhero vision and he loves getting assists!

10 BRUMA
Rapid winger blessed with quick feet, a sweet right foot and loads of tricks!

FACTBOX
CLUB:
Galatasaray

COUNTRY:
Portugal

BORN:
Bissau, Guinea-Bissau

AGE:
18

POSITION:
Winger

DID YOU KNOW? He was second top scorer at this year's Under-20 World Cup!

POTENTIAL VALUE!
£35 MILLION

PLAYING STYLE
Portugal certainly know a thing or two about producing wingers – and this is the new kid on the scene. He's got the tricks of Nani, the pace of Ronaldo and within 30 yards of goal, it's danger time for keepers!

9 ERIK LAMELA
Epic dribbler who cuts in from the right and unleashes hell with his left foot!

FACTBOX
CLUB:
Tottenham

COUNTRY:
Argentina

BORN:
Buenos Aires, Argentina

AGE:
21

POSITION:
Forward

DID YOU KNOW? He turned down Barcelona when he was just 12 years old!

POTENTIAL VALUE!
£45 MILLION

PLAYING STYLE
Erik has been called the Argentine Cristiano Ronaldo, and not because he throws a tantrum when he gets tackled. He dribbled past opponents 99 times last season – 40 more than the man he replaced, Gareth Bale!

8 VIKTOR FISCHER

Expect the unexpected from this teenage match-winning forward!

FACTBOX

CLUB:
Ajax

COUNTRY:
Denmark

BORN:
Aarhus,
Denmark

AGE:
19

POSITION:
Winger

POTENTIAL VALUE!

£45 MILLION

DID YOU KNOW?
He scored 20 goals in 30 games for Denmark under-17s!

PLAYING STYLE : This deadly Dane has quick feet and an even quicker mind. Whether he's latching onto a through-ball, cutting in from the wing or simply twisting and turning inside the penalty area, he was born to score!

---

7 ALEX OXLADE-CHAMBERLAIN

Direct, explosive dribbler who's got a right foot like a sledgehammer!

FACTBOX

CLUB:
Arsenal

COUNTRY:
England

BORN:
Portsmouth,
England

AGE:
20

POSITION:
Midfielder

POTENTIAL VALUE!

£45 MILLION

DID YOU KNOW?
His senior school didn't play football so he had to play rugby!

PLAYING STYLE : Bursting with energy and self-confidence, nothing fazes The Ox. He gets the ball, he beats a man, then he beats another, and then another, and then, BANG, before you can say his name, the ball's in the net!

6 MARCO VERRATTI

Classy playmaker who orchestrates everything from the centre-circle!

FACTBOX

CLUB:
PSG

COUNTRY:
Italy

BORN:
Pescara, Italy

AGE:
20

POSITION:
Midfielder

DID YOU KNOW? He had a 90% passing accuracy last season for PSG!

POTENTIAL VALUE!
£45 MILLION

PLAYING STYLE
If you gave Italian legend Andrea Pirlo a good shave, chopped off his flowing locks and made him 14 years younger, you'd have this kid – a little pass master who's going to be a huge star for many years to come!

5 JULIAN DRAXLER

Creative midfielder who can change a game with a moment of magic!

FACTBOX

CLUB:
Schalke

COUNTRY:
Germany

BORN:
Gladbeck, Germany

AGE:
20

POSITION:
Midfielder

DID YOU KNOW? His favourite book is England hero David Beckham's autobiography!

POTENTIAL VALUE!
£50 MILLION

PLAYING STYLE
Oh, what a surprise, another German who's flamin' brilliant at football! This young lad is a bundle of explosiveness – he likes to get it onto his hammer of a right foot before walloping a shot at goal!

4 GERARD DEULOFEU

Skilful forward who ghosts past defenders and is ace at one-on-ones!

Everton 18 78

FACTBOX

CLUB:
**Everton
(on loan from
Barcelona)**

COUNTRY:
Spain

BORN:
**Riudarenes,
Spain**

AGE:
19

POSITION:
Forward

DID YOU KNOW? Gerard has been at Barca's famous academy since he was nine!

POTENTIAL VALUE!
£55 MILLION

PLAYING STYLE : There are some things the Spanish excel at – paella, massive tomato fights and producing twinkle-toed attacking midfielders. The whisper around the corridors of the Nou Camp is that this guy is the new Messi!

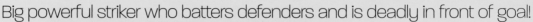

3 ROMELU LUKAKU

Big powerful striker who batters defenders and is deadly in front of goal!

Everton 18 78

FACTBOX

CLUB:
**Everton
(on loan from
Chelsea)**

COUNTRY:
Belgium

BORN:
**Antwerp,
Belgium**

AGE:
20

POSITION:
Striker

DID YOU KNOW? Romelu scored 76 goals in 34 games for his under-12 team!

POTENTIAL VALUE!
£60 MILLION

PLAYING STYLE : How on earth this guy is still only 20 is as scary as it is baffling. He's already played loads for Belgium and is, quite simply, a beast who leaves defenders cowering for their mummy after 90 minutes of bruising action!

2 RAPHAEL VARANE
Stylish, speedy centre-back who's an expert at snuffing out attacks!

FACTBOX

CLUB:
Real Madrid

COUNTRY:
France

BORN:
Lille, France

AGE:
20

POSITION:
Centre-back

DID YOU KNOW? Varane is the Spanish club's tallest outfield player at 6ft 3in!

POTENTIAL VALUE!
£50 MILLION

PLAYING STYLE This kid burst onto the scene last season – and Real fans couldn't believe what they were seeing. He's got the pace of a forward, the skills of a midfielder, the heart of a lion and the potential to be a world-beater!

1 PAUL POGBA
An epic combination of power, pace, creativity and bazooka shooting!

FACTBOX

CLUB:
Juventus

COUNTRY:
France

BORN:
Lagny-Sur-Marne, France

AGE:
20

POSITION:
Midfielder

DID YOU KNOW? He spent three years at Man. United, before joining Juve last year!

POTENTIAL VALUE!
£80 MILLION

PLAYING STYLE Pogba's athletic, dynamic and, at 6ft 2in, a real powerhouse. He transforms from midfield enforcer one second to silky-skilled playmaker the next – and that's why he's the No.1 star of the future!

odd one out!

It's a quiz classic – you've simply got to work out who is the odd one out from the selection of four below!

1 DIFFICULTY: EASY!

AN AMAZONIAN TREE FROG

COFFEE-FLAVOURED ICE CREAM

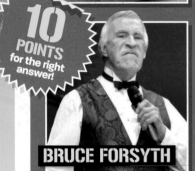

BRUCE FORSYTH

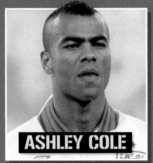

ASHLEY COLE

10 POINTS for the right answer!

THE ODD ONE OUT IS: _Answer_

2 DIFFICULTY: MEDIUM!

ZLATAN IBRAHIMOVIC

1970s POP GROUP ABBA

A MOOSE

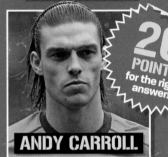

ANDY CARROLL

20 POINTS for the right answer!

THE ODD ONE OUT IS: _Answer_

3 DIFFICULTY: HARD!

GARETH BALE

THEO WALCOTT

ALEX OXLADE-CHAMBERLAIN

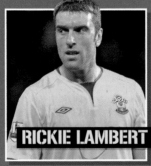

RICKIE LAMBERT

30 POINTS for the right answer!

THE ODD ONE OUT IS: _Lambert_

4 DIFFICULTY: ROCK-SOLID!

PETER CROUCH

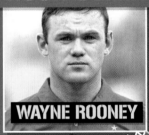

WAYNE ROONEY

JERMAIN DEFOE

STEVEN GERRARD

40 POINTS for the right answer!

THE ODD ONE OUT IS: _Rooney_

MY SCORE ☐ OUT OF **100**

ANSWERS ON p92

TURN TO p90 FOR MORE QUIZ ACTION!

LIONEL MESSI

The childhood secrets of the world's best-ever player!

This is where the world's best player grew up!

LEO WAS BORN IN ROSARIO, the third biggest city in Argentina, on 24 June, 1987. He was a chubby little baby but immediately had a skill for one particular game – and it wasn't football. No, Little Messi was the family champion at marbles!

HE WAS A LITTLE STAR ON THE PITCH BUT OFF IT HE WAS INCREDIBLY SHY. At school, he'd sit at the back of the class, silently. He hated maths – but loved PE and Art. He was so small his brother Rodrigo called him The Flea!

Little Leo lines up for his junior team Grandoli!

HE WAS HOT PROPERTY – NOT JUST IN ARGENTINA. Barcelona scouts knew all about him too. When he was 13, they invited him over to Spain for a trial but, despite impressing, the Barca management thought he was too small to be a football player!

Leo's a legend in Rosario. That's the mayor and his mum!

When he was nine, he scored 100 goals in a season!

Messi moved to La Masia academy 13 years ago!

SINCE THE AGE OF TEN, Leo had been having injections every day to help him grow. These jabs cost £90k per year. The Barcelona directors were eventually persuaded to sign him and they also agreed to pay for his treatment and for his entire family to move to Spain!

HE DIDN'T HAVE A FOOTY TEAM UNTIL HIS GRAN ORDERED THE LOCAL COACH TO PLAY 7-YEAR-OLD LIONEL. The coach laughed because Leo was so small, but he eventually agreed and watched on in amazement as Leo skipped past defenders twice his size – every time he got the ball!

AFTER THREE YEARS WITH HIS FIRST TEAM GRANDOLI he signed for Newell's Old Boys. He scored more than 100 goals a season for them and it wasn't long before he was being labeled the new Maradona!

The home of Newell's Old Boys!

The rest, as they say, is history!

FROM LITTLE LEO TO HUGE SUPERSTAR!

Magic Messi's last five seasons for Barcelona

2008-09: 51 games, 38 goals!

2009-10: 53 games, 47 goals!

2010-11: 55 games, 53 goals!

2011-12: 60 games, 73 goals!

2012-13: 50 games, 60 goals!

⟫⟫⟫ SUBSCRIPTION OFFER! ⟫⟫⟫

Subscribe to **MATCH OF THE DAY** magazine and you'll...

GET FOUR ISSUES FOR £1!

4 reasons to subscribe today!

1 PAY ONLY £1 for your first 4 issues!

3 FREE UK DELIVERY to your door every week

2 SAVE 20% on the cover price!

4 NEVER MISS AN ISSUE of your fave footy mag!

2 easy ways to subscribe

1 PHONE

the hotline now on
0844 844 0263
quoting MDPANN13

2 VISIT

our subscriptions website at
www.buysubscriptions.com/motd
and enter code MDPANN13

2 You won't get this!

How many of these stars have played for an English Premier League team?

misung best nonett

3 Crikey, I've got it!

Who is this powerful Premier League striker?

b payne/te

6 Wow! That's tough!

West Brom's Billy Jones was the only Englishman to do what last season?

Scoke work

gram

12 **13** **14** **15**

cavanty *oxpon* *wyctp* *sheflue*

MY SCORE
15 OUT OF **150**

ANSWERS ON p92

Quiz answers!

Are you a quiz champ or a quiz chump? Now's the time to find out!

Quiz 1 FROM PAGE 12
True or false?

1 False,
2 False,
3 False,
4 True,
5 True

MY SCORE ☐ OUT OF **50**

Quiz 2 FROM PAGE 42
Crossword

MY SCORE ☐ OUT OF **60**

Quiz 3 FROM PAGE 72
Who are ya?

1 Jonny Evans,
2 Seamus Coleman,
3 Jonas Olsson,
4 Gaston Ramirez,
5 Leon Britton,
6 Kyle Naughton,
7 James Morrison,
8 Winston Reid,
9 Nacho Monreal,
10 Andreas Weimann,
11 Glenn Whelan,
12 Cesar Azpilicueta,
13 Joe Allen,
14 Craig Bellamy,
15 Matija Nastasic,
16 Davide Santon,
17 Wes Hoolahan,
18 Steve Sidwell,
19 Mike Williamson,
20 Robert Snodgrass

MY SCORE ☐ OUT OF **40**

Quiz 4 FROM PAGE 82
Odd one out!

1 Ashley Cole: none of the others have over 100 caps for England
2 Andy Carroll: all of the others are Swedish
3 Rickie Lambert: all of the others started their career at Southampton
4 Wayne Rooney: all of the others have scored for England at a World Cup.

MY SCORE ☐ OUT OF **100**

Quiz 4 FROM PAGE 90
Genius round

1 Nikodem,
2 Four,
3 Christian Benteke, 4 West Ham, 5 Anfield,
6 Score a goal for West Brom,
7 Leeds,
8 Bolton,
9 Plymouth,
10 Ipswich,
11 Wolves,
12 Coventry,
13 Oxford,
14 Wycombe,
15 Sheffield Wednesday.

MY SCORE ☐ OUT OF **150**

MY FINAL SCORE
☐ OUT OF **400**

WHAT'S YOUR SCORE?

0-19	20-99	100-199	200-299	300-400
Uh-oh! That's a spectacular fail. Even a donkey would have done better than that!	It's back to footy school for you, dude – that score is just not good enough, I'm afraid!	You're getting there. A solid score but there's certainly room for improvement!	Now we're talking! That was a quality display – you delivered under massive pressure!	Wow! That was quite simply world class. You are the RVP of the quiz world!

Planet Footy
PAGE 26-27

MATCH OF THE DAY MAGAZINE

SUAREZ

VAN PERSIE

BAINES

WILSHERE

MATA

OFFICIAL!

THE BEST-SELLING FOOTY MAG IN THE UK!

MATCH OF THE DAY

Write to us at...
Match Of The Day magazine
Immediate Media, Vineyard
House, 44 Brook Green,
Hammersmith,
London, W6 7BT

Telephone 020 7150 5121
Email shout@motdmag.com
www.motdmag.com

Annual editor	Mark Parry	Picture editor	Liz Peel
Annual art editor	Paul Carpenter	Production editor	Neil Queen-Jones
Match Of The Day editor	Ian Foster	Sub-editor	Joe Shackley
Art editor	Blue Buxton	Publishing consultant	Jaynie Bye
Deputy art editor	Lee Midwinter	Editorial director	Corinna Shaffer
Features editor	Ed Bearryman	Annual images	PA Photos
Senior writer	Richard Clare	Thanks to	Gary Lineker, Alan Shearer,
Group picture editor	Natasha Thompson		Alan Hansen, Mark Chapman,
Picture editor	Jason Timson		Mark Lawrenson, Dan Walker,
			Paul Armstrong, Paul Cemmick.

First published in 2013 by BBC Books, an imprint of Ebury Publishing. A Random House Group
Company. Copyright © Match Of The Day magazine 2013. All rights reserved. No part of
this publication may be reproduced, stored in a retrieval system, or transmitted in any form
or by any means, electronic, mechanical, photocopying, recording or otherwise, without the
prior permission of the copyright owner. The Random House Group Limited Reg. No.
954009. Addresses for companies within the Random House Group can be found at www.
randomhouse.co.uk. A CIP catalogue record for this book is available from the British Library.
ISBN: 978 1 849 90673 9. Commissioning editor: Albert DePetrillo, project editor: Joe Cottington,
Production: Phil Spencer. Printed and bound in Germany by Mohn Media GmbH. To buy books
by your favourite authors and register for offers visit www.randomhouse.co.uk.

BBC

The licence to publish this magazine was acquired from BBC Worldwide by
Immediate Media Company on 1 November 2011. We remain committed to making
a magazine of the highest editorial quality, one that complies with BBC editorial
and commercial guidelines and connects with BBC programmes.

Match Of The Day Magazine is published by Immediate Media Company
London Limited, under licence from BBC Worldwide Limited.
© Immediate Media Company London Limited, 2013.

5 HEADLINES WE WANT TO READ IN 2014!

IT'S DR ROO

ENGLAND striker Wayne Rooney was last night unveiled as the new Dr Who by BBC bosses.

TIME LORD

Wazza — best known for tackling defenders rather than Cybermen — said he was over the moon to be named as the thirteenth Time Lord. "I'm over the moon to be named as the thirteenth Time Lord," he said.

EDAM HAZARD

THE WORLD of football was in shock today after Chelsea manager Jose Mourinho confirmed winger Eden Hazard is made of cheese.

The Belgium star underwent urgent medical tests at the club's training ground yesterday after sprouting mould and giving off a strange smell.

CHEESE

A Chelsea source said: "Whenever he walks into the dressing room the lads start signing For Cheese A Jolly Good Fellow!"